# THE CHURCH

# THE CHURCH

Prayers of Celebration

SAINT ANDREW PRESS
Edinburgh

First published in 2010 by
SAINT ANDREW PRESS
121 George Street
Edinburgh EH2 4YN

Copyright © Saint Andrew Press, 2010

ISBN 978 0 7152 0948 6

The right of the Office for Worship and Doctrine, Mission and
Discipleship Council of the Church of Scotland to be identified
as author of this work has been asserted in accordance with the
Copyright, Designs and Patents Act 1988.

**British Library Cataloguing in Publication Data**
A catalogue record for this book is available from the British Library

It is the Publisher's policy to only use papers that are natural and
recyclable and that have been manufactured from timber grown in
renewable, properly managed forests. All of the manufacturing
processes of the papers are expected to conform to the environmental
regulations of the country of origin.

Typeset by Waverley Typesetters, Warham, Norfolk
Printed and bound in Great Britian by Bell & Bain Ltd, Glasgow

# Contents

# How to use this book

The prayers in this collection celebrate the church in its many forms, from the call of the disciples, to mission and evangelism and ecumenism, to church buildings. We consider congregations and office holders and Bible characters. We think about the hopes and the joy and the frustration and the many other emotions that are part of church life. Each prayer is rooted in scripture, and each addresses a contemporary issue relevant to today's life.

You can start at the beginning and work your way to the end, or you can look through the prayers to find a particular topic you would like to address at a particular time, or you can simply pick a prayer at random and reflect on its theme. The chosen path is entirely up to you.

Some of the prayers have Scripture Readings, which are there for further reflection or to allow prayer groups to discuss the themes in relation to both the scriptures and the contemporary world.

There are some prayer activities, too. These are designed to stimulate your many senses in a prayerful way. They are perhaps best used when you are alone, when you have some time away from the routine of daily life. It may be useful to create a 'prayer corner': some personal place where you can have as much peace and quiet for reflection as you possibly can. The prayer activities hope to prompt a personal response; but prayer groups also may find that they are appropriate. You are, of course, encouraged to be creative with them, to adapt them to your own circumstances. The point is to engage with prayer, not to let it be a dull ritual.

We hope that these prayers help you to approach church with renewed or affirmed enthusiasm.

# Introduction

The church is a place of celebration and also a people of celebration.

What is there in your life to celebrate? What is there in the lives of the people you know to celebrate?

The church is where we come together with people we might not always choose. Ponder the wonder of God's love bringing us together, helping us to appreciate the different gifts and personalities we all have. Pray for our own Church community. Pray also for the wider Church, this worldwide network that unites us.

Let the food you eat, and the books you read, remind you of the other parts of God's world and how we are all connected.

# The Church

*With this great crowd of witnesses around us ...*

~ Hebrews 12:1 ~

Lord of the Church,
The place we go each week to meet with you formally.
Not to tie you to one building
As if all the majesty and glory that overflows the heavens
Could be contained within four stone walls on Earth!

But our Church,
The place where life and death are celebrated.

Our Church,
The place of baptism and new beginning,
Of family and growth; of learning and sharing, of singing
and silence.

Our Church,
The place of sermon and teaching, where your Word is
faithfully passed on
For us to meditate upon, be challenged by, struggle with,
puzzle over.

Our Church,
The place where bread and wine remind us of that once for
   all event,
Where broken body and spilled blood brought salvation to
   a believing world.

Our Church,
Where marriage bells peal, and funeral bells toll.

Our Church,
Where family and friends gather in the wider family.

Our Church,
Where ancient songs and modern hymns
And flowers and fabrics
And tears and joy
Weave together to make the tapestry we know as
   Our Church.

Lord of the Church,
   Lord of our Church,
Lead us and bless us,
With the power of Christ.

## Readings

Exodus 3:1–6; 1 Kings 8:6–21; Psalm 100; Luke 4:16–21;
Acts 11:19–26; Revelation 21:22–7

# 'I am there among them'

~ Matthew 18:20 ~

## Prayer for Reflection

What can one person do?
... I sometimes ask, Lord,
as if worship and mission
     and spreading the Gospel
     and renewing the church
     and feeding the hungry
     and clothing the naked
     and protecting the environment
     and making peace
were all solo activities.

Help me,
who here prays to you on my own,
to live for you
in the company of the very different others
who are your friends,
and among whom you have promised to meet me.

## Prayer on Today's Theme

Where two or three are gathered
... in a small church in a lonely glen;
... in a large church in a lonely city;
... in a corner of a country
    where Christians are threatened;
... in deserts or jungles or outbacks
    where meeting places are few;
... outside a hospital ward
    waiting for the theatre door to open;
... around a bed
    at the time for last farewells;
where two or three are gathered
in your name,
may they treasure the time
and know your presence.

# 'I am with you always, to the End of Time'

~ Matthew 28:20 ~

### Prayer for Reflection

Ah, Jesus,
if I met you on a train
and heard just a snippet of your conversation,
I would ask countless questions
until we parted company.

I would be so excited
to meet and make such a unique friend;
every second would be precious.

Just because you have promised
to be with me to the end of time,
don't let me take you for granted,
or fail to show the enthusiasm
which would be so evident
if we met only for a few hours
on a train.

### Prayer on Today's Theme

Today, Lord,
I pray for those at the end . . .
at the end of their tether, wondering what next;
at the end of a relationship, wondering what next;
at the end of their employment, wondering what next;
at the end of their life, with the same wondering.

Whatever happens next,
may those threatened by the future
find in you faith enough for today;
and know that it comes from the one
who is already in tomorrow.

We pray today for those who are committed to sharing the
scriptures and the deepening the devotional life of people at
home and abroad, that the seed may fall on fertile soil and
yield a good harvest for their Lord.

# 'I am the Vine; you are the Branches'

~ John 15:5 ~

## Prayer for Reflection

Unless
I remain
united
to you,
I can bear no fruit.

Unless
I allow myself
to be pruned
by you,
I cannot be more fruitful.

You said it, Lord,
so I must take it seriously.

## Prayer on Today's Theme

Lord, keep us together
    as your church,

especially when we become
obsessed with our differences,
or put fund-raising before faith.

Keep us together
when we disagree about favourite hymns;
when some want to protest for peace
and others want to hold a praise evening.

Keep us together;
and let our tensions be creative
only and because we are all rooted in you.

⟶⊚

Mingle, O God,
our humanity with your divinity,
your greatness with our humility,
and our humility with your greatness,
through Jesus Christ our Lord.

~ *St Gregory of Armenia* ~

# *Growing*

*They are like trees planted by streams of water, which yields their fruit in its season.*

~ Psalm 1:3 ~

Lord, just as Solomon built the Temple from cedars
You invite me
to allow you to build your temple within me.
Just as Solomon ordered the best wood, the Cedars of
    Lebanon
May I grow
the best I can for you, straight and strong

Just as the cedars embodied your majesty
You invite me
to let your love be in every fibre of my very being.
Just as the cedars spoke to people of your glory
May I let
your light shine through me

Just as their wood created sacred space
You invite me
to be moulded to create more room for your Presence.
Just as their wood exuded a beautiful smell

May I bring
the fragrance of your love to others

Following Jesus, who helps us understand that our bodies
    are temples
of the living God.    AMEN.

## Prayer Activity

Become aware of your breathing and your heartbeat. Reflect
on the miracle that so much happens in your body without
your needing to be conscious of the detail. Reflect that God
has placed the Holy Spirit within you that works without
your needing to understand also, creating a temple for the
Living God.

# Builders of the Temple

*Unless the Lord builds the house, those who build it labour in vain.*

~ Psalm 127:1 ~

Lord, we thank you for those sacred places
    where your Word is declared, your Sacraments
      administered,
    when we sensed that you were there, when a
      fellowship was enjoyed,
    where and when we really worshipped you,
where and when your grace was given.
We thank you for the many whose giving and doing built
   the churches of our land;
for the many whose praising, preaching and praying
   hallowed their walls;
for the many who in times past built our towns and cities:
architects and engineers, masons and bricklayers, and
   many more.

Recalling those who, with Nehemiah, restored the Temple
   of Jerusalem,
raise up in our day builders like Nehemiah's
to repair and to create new sacred spaces.
Strengthen us to be the Church without walls,

breaking through barriers for the good of the Gospel.

Make us living stones in that great enterprise.

Lord, as we commend to you all who strive for a Jerusalem
on earth:

statesmen and sociologists, economists and planners of all
kinds;

watch over the watchmen: those in the police and
emergency services;

and strengthen the hands of those who would do a good
work for your Kingdom. AMEN.

### Prayer Activity

Remember the children's question, 'Are you a stumbling block
or a stepping stone?' Or, 'Are you a real brick?' Think how
you may help others and the Other; how you might play a
better part in the fabric of society and in building up the
Church – and don't be afraid of being used!

# *Rebuilding*

*Then the Word of the Lord came by the prophet Haggai, saying: Is it a time for you yourselves to live in your panelled houses, while this house lies in ruins? Go up to the hills and bring wood and build the house, so that I may take pleasure in it and be honoured, says the Lord.*

~ Haggai 1:3, 4, 8 ~

Lord,
There are times when you question our priorities,
When you challenge our complacency;
And undermine our desire for comfort.

As once you summoned your people from their selfish
    preoccupations
To the urgent task of re-building the temple,
So also you call us to the hallowed work of rebuilding and
    renewal.

You summon us to rebuild that which is in ruins,
To mend that which has been broken, and to heal that
    which has been hurt.

As once you called the people to work together, to labour
    on the ruins, family with family,
And neighbour with neighbour,
So you call us to the Kingdom's work.

Today I pray for the unity of the Church
In pursuing the common vision of a healed world:
The earth filled with your glory as the waters cover the sea.

## Prayer Activity

Take time to reflect on the theme of rebuilding. In your own congregation: what needs rebuilding? (Conversely, what needs to be demolished?) What is broken or hurting? Have you contributed to that hurt or brokenness? Reflect on how you can be part of the rebuilding/healing process.

You can do the same reflection in relation to your own family and community.

# Our Spiritual Home

> How lovely is your dwelling place,
> O Lord of hosts!
> My soul longs, indeed it faints
> for the courts of the Lord;
> my heart and my flesh sing for joy
> to the living God.
>
> ~ Psalm 84:1–2 ~

Lord, I must confess to being fond of 'my church':
I love the familiar order of service, the older tunes and
   hymns,
(the 'hymn-sandwich'!)
the children going out to Sunday School.
There's so much that is dear to me:
my place in the corner of that pew,
the elders coming round with Communion, the folks that
   are glad to see me.
*I was glad when they said to me, 'Let us go to the house of the
   Lord!'*

But I know that your presence is not confined to the
   church.
Vast! Infinite! Words fail me!
The mind can only grasp a little,
   the heart takes in only a raindrop, of your cosmic love.

*Even the sparrow finds a home,*
*and the swallow a nest for herself,*
*where she may lay her young,*
*at your altars, O Lord of hosts,*
*my King and my God.*

Yes! Like the sparrow
(now threatened with extinction) returning to her nest,
in church the soul finds joy,
her instinct blessed.    AMEN.

*Pray for the peace of Jerusalem:*
*'May they prosper who love you ...'*
*For the sake of my relatives and friends*
*I will say, 'Peace be within you.'*
*For the sake of the house of the Lord our God,*
*I will seek your good.*

# The Church – a Gift

*Now you are the body of Christ and individually members of it.*
~ 1 Corinthians 12:27 ~

Lord – your church a gift?
Sometimes I look around and cannot believe I'm here!
Can this really be what you meant?
My fellow Christians are so different from me.
They are full of awkward edges.
They don't always seem to have got it quite right.
Must I love them all and carry their burdens?

And what of the wider church?
Sometimes tradition seems to overtake compassion,
bigotry and intolerance take the place of acceptance,
divisions give the lie to the message of reconciliation.

Yet you have called us to be a *sign*
of the true community that God plans for the world;
and as the word of God is preached, believed and obeyed,
we are shaped into an *instrument* for bringing it to pass;
and as we share in communion at the table of Jesus
    Christ
we become a *foretaste* of the reconciled life in God's
    kingdom.

Grant that as Christ's body we may see diversity as a gift,
and so challenge a world where differences are taken as cue
for conflict.

Grant that our awkward shapes may fit together to build
strong walls of a temple to your glory.

Grant that we may live in our traditions and customs in
such away

that we are continually open to the renewing of your Holy
Spirit.

### Prayer Activity

Call to mind your local church. What is your immediate
image of it? Rows of people in pews? A solid stone building?
Re-imagine your church using some of the images above.
Choose one of them, e.g. vine, bride, body, wedding party,
and think of the way your church would link together, move,
react, pray if that were the only possible picture of how things
should be.

# Mission

*Send out your light and your truth to be my guide; let them lead me to your holy hill, to your dwelling place.*

~ Psalm 43:3 ~

### Prayer for Reflection

If I met you, Jesus Christ,
I might not think that you were on
a mission.

Your talk would be of common
and curious things:    salt, dough,
lost lambs, lost coins,
paying taxes, hosting a meal,
wise virgins,
and foolish house-builders.

I would not know you were on a mission,
I would think you were making sense of life,
lighting up the ordinary, identifying the truth.

When next you look with compassion on the world
and need mission done in your way,
Lord, send me.

## Prayer on Today's Theme

God of all nations,
whose Church blossoms in lands
once considered barren,
and whose name is holy in every tongue,
set alight with your love
us in the once Christian West
whose zeal can hardly smoulder.

Where we have sent missionaries,
      make us keen to receive them;
where we have taught the world,
      make us keen to learn from it:
where we have presented our Lord in our image,
      let us receive him as seen by other eyes.

We ask this because world mission is not ours,
it is Christ's;
and we are part of the world in need of awakening.

# Apostles at Pentecost

*In the last days it will be, God declares, that I will pour out my Spirit upon all flesh, and your sons and your daughters shall prophesy, and your young men shall see visions, and your old men shall dream dreams.*

~ Acts 2:17 ~

Lord, I praise you for Pentecost
when fearful and faltering apostles
caught the hint of a new fragrance.
I praise you for those who knew
the south wind of your spirit,
breathing hope of Spring and new beginnings
into hearts clamped in Winter's grip
of agonising shame and failure.

I praise you that ordinary, all-too-frail
human beings just like me
realised to their utter astonishment
that they were no longer slaves
to the crippling pain of yesterday,
but were now liberated
into the energising promise of tomorrow.

I praise you for their discovery
that the last word

is not one of defeat but of victory,
that the Word that echoes into all eternity
is not 'My God, My God, why have you forsaken me?'
but 'Christ is risen – he is risen indeed!'

Today, Lord, I pray for the Church,
that we might take your springtime
into a world still in winter's grip.

# Joy – the Church Grows

*And day by day the Lord added new converts to their number.*
~ Acts 2:47 ~

Lord Jesus Christ,
we pray for growth in the Church –
banishing apathy,
bringing individuals new blessing,
making society whole.
May your kingdom come.

Lord Jesus Christ, we pray for
a deepening of faith
a strengthening of relationships,
And grace to perceive your life in others.

May the signs and wonders of your kingdom
bring life and growth
to our Church
and our world.    AMEN.

### Readings

Isaiah 55:1–9; Acts 2:44–7; 1 Corinthians 3:5–9; Galatians
5:22–4

### Prayer Activity

Put on some music and dance, or imagine dancing. Let
your body pray by moving and reveal to you that it is the
dwelling-place of God and the Holy Spirit. Let yourself be
drawn into the dance.

### Lord's Prayer

### Blessing

Now to him who is able through the power
which is at work among us
to do immeasurably more than
all we can ask or conceive,
to him be glory in the church
and in Christ Jesus
from generation to generation
for evermore!   AMEN.
~ *Ephesians 3:20–1* ~

# The Early Church

*Now I appeal to you, brothers and sisters, by the name of our Lord Jesus Christ, that all of you be in agreement and that there be no divisions among you, but that you be united in the same mind and the same purpose.*

~ 1 Corinthians 1:10 ~

Loving God, how long will you put up with us?
You left no written instructions for your Church, but you
    did leave us your example.
How have we become so divided?
What are we to make of a Church of 30,000 denominations
    world-wide,
each claiming to be your true body?

Nevertheless, what richness in this diversity! –
different people, different gifts, different opportunities.
Help us to build on our differences, trusting that your
    Spirit is at work in us all
and that your message is being carried to all the corners of
    the world.

Where along the way we have lost the enthusiasm, the
    insight, the courage to break new ground shown in
    the life of the young Church, help us to hear from

one another and to hear your Word so that we recover the Gospel which is new every morning and feel the presence of Christ with us as vividly as they did on the first Easter day.

## Readings

|                          |                                     |
|-------------------------:|:------------------------------------|
| 1 Corinthians 1          | *Divisions in the church*           |
| Acts 4:32–7              | *Believers share their possessions* |
| 1 Corinthians 10:23–11:1 | *Do all to the glory of God*        |
| 2 Corinthians 4:16–5:10  | *Living by faith*                   |

## Prayer Activity

Sit quietly, breathe deeply, let your mind move around the area you live and think of all the churches found in it. Ask God to breathe his Holy Spirit on each church and the people who worship and witness there week by week.

# Service

*I shall choose for my companions the faithful in the land; my servants will be those whose lives are blameless.*

~ Psalm 101:6 ~

### Prayer for Reflection

All-knowing God,
if I cannot break bread,
    let me bake bread;
if I cannot lend a hand,
    let me take a hand;
if I cannot say a prayer,
    let me answer a prayer;
if I cannot light a candle,
    let me be a light;
if I cannot sit and serve
    let me stand and wait.

For it seems,
by all accounts,
that there are many members
    but one body,
many ways of serving,
    but one Lord.

## Prayer on Today's Theme

In a previous age, when the demands of your Gospel
were recognised, to the needs of our nation
your people responded in the building of schools,
     the clothing of the poor,
     the care of the sick,
and in the protests to end slavery,
child labour, and oppressive working conditions.

In this age,
living in a different order though under the same skies,
make your Church able to discern your call to care.
When we see the drug addict,
     the hopeless youth,
     the Aids victim,
     the rape victim,
calling for our time and attention,
may we not be quick to walk to the other side,
lest, when our eyes least expect it,
we see you, Lord Christ,
moving in the opposite direction.

# The Local Church (1)

*How dearly loved is your dwelling place!*
*I pine and faint with longing*
*for the courts of the Lord's Temple.*

~ Psalm 84:1 ~

## Prayer for Reflection

Thank you Lord
for the Church –
>    the church in which I was baptised
>    the church in which I was reared
>    the church in which I was confirmed
>    the church in which I am a member.

Forgive me
if I have been quick to criticise in it
the faults which are also in me.
Forgive me
if I have expected of it
more than I have ever given to it.
Forgive me
if I have continually seen that church as an 'it'
and not as a community of your people.

## Prayer on Today's Theme

Today, Lord,
I remember my local church ...
    my minister ...
    my elder ...
and ask you to bless them.

Today I remember those I always sit beside
    and any who are strangers,
and ask you to make us one.

Today I remember the needs of my local church
    and its great potentials,
and ask for their fulfilment.

Today I remember how much I give to my local church and
   ask you if it is enough.

# The Local Church (2)

*Let the world of Christ dwell in you richly.*
~ Colossians 3:16 ~

### Prayer for Ourselves

When I first came to faith I sang with enthusiasm
'I'm not ashamed to own my Lord'.
Now I know there is more to it.
Listening to others is demanding, sharing their hurts takes
a lot out of me,
praying can be a real struggle, working alongside others
can use up all your patience.
Yet, Lord,

the more the challenges unfold, the more you bring me the
joy
of discovering new springs of faith and of growing to
greater maturity in your service.

### Prayer for Others

Lord Jesus,
be with all ministers and deacons;
give them strength and encouragement, enthusiasm and
inspiration,

as they seek to guide their congregations.
Be with all who are elders;
guide them in their care of your people,
and give them the joy of truly working together
as they plan for the good of your church.
Be with all who teach the young;
give them the grace to remember,
as they seek to prove to them your love
and nurture their growing love for you, that they were once
    children too.
Grant to all congregations
the grace of welcoming others, courage to take risks,
confidence in declaring your love, the joy of giving true
    praise.

# The World Church (1)

*God the Lord has spoken and summoned the world from the rising of the sun to its setting.*

~ Psalm 50:1 ~

## Prayer for Reflection

When you called me
to be a Christian, Lord,
you did not tell me the size of your family.

You did not say
that many speak no English,
that many have no sanctuary,
    no choir,
    no organ,
that some depict you as a black man,
that some dance joyfully
and others use no words in worship.

To think that I am related
to such a diverse family!
To think that you knew all the time,
but kept it a surprise!

## Prayer on Today's Theme

Where today
your church is in danger . . . . . . . . . . . . . protect it;
where today
your church is too comfortable . . . . . . . . . . . . . disturb it.
Where today
your church stands with the poor . . . . . . . . . . . . . affirm it;
where today
your church hides behind the rich . . . . . . . . . . . . . confront it.
Where today
your church proclaims its risen Lord . . . . . . . . . . . . . fill it
   with your love;
where today
your church seeks to serve itself . . . . . . . . . . . . . let it know
   your displeasure.

⁓◎⁓

O Lord our God,
listening to us here,
you accept also the prayers of our brothers and sisters
in Africa, Asia, the Pacific, the Americas, and Europe.
We are all one in prayer.

So may we, as one, rightly carry out your commission
to witness and to love
in the Church and throughout the world.

Accept our prayers graciously
even when they are somewhat strange.
They are offered in Jesus' name.

*~ A Prayer from the Ghanaian Church ~*

# The World Church (2)

*Live in love, as Christ loved us and gave himself up for us.*

~ Ephesians 5:2 ~

## Prayer for Ourselves

I am proud to be a member of my church.
I like to sit in my seat on Sunday mornings,
surrounded by friends,
listening to words of comfort,
joining in songs of praise.
How lovely is thy dwelling place to me!

But there are other ways to worship you.
Not all places of worship are beautiful.
Many worshippers are in danger
     when they meet to praise you.
Let me never be so complacent
that I discount those who worship
     differently from me,
or believe my church to be the only true one.

### Prayer for Others

I pray for all the branches of the worldwide church:
when they wrestle with issues in their society,
when they find themselves in the midst of ethnic conflict,
when their leaders are tried and gaoled,
when their faith is threatened by hardship and famine,
when a dominant religion makes life difficult.
Show me how I might offer strength to them,
and help them to trust in the strength
      that their fellowship in Christ brings.
I pray for my congregation,
that it may be ready to learn from other Christians.
In singing hymns from other lands and in praying for their
   needs,
may we be renewed in our understanding of the faith
and revived in service to the community.

# *Worship*

*From the rising of the sun to its setting may the Lord's name be praised.*

~ Psalm 113:3 ~

### Prayer for Reflection

Every minute
of every hour of every day,
by the Church on earth
and the Church in heaven,
your praise is sung,
your name is hallowed, your grace is enjoyed.

So, Lord,
when in these brief moments,
1 focus my mind on you,
1 am not alone;
I am in the company of countless millions
using angel tongues and human language.
And, more marvellous yet,

in the midst of this feast of worship,
you hear my voice and heed my prayer.

Hallowed be your name!

## Prayer on Today's Theme

For those who lead worship week by week,
lest they weary or grow stale … your encouragement, Lord.
For those who write hymns, plan liturgies,
lest they become predictable … your inspiration, Lord.
For those who cannot make it to church
and who must worship alone … your company, Lord.
For those who seek new ways to enable the unchurched
to discover how to pray … your insight, Lord.

And to all who will attend worship next Sunday,
give a spirit of expectation;
let them find much to offer,
and discover that you have much to give.

# *Evangelism*

*The coming generation will be told of the Lord; they will make known his righteous deeds, declaring to a people yet unborn, 'The Lord has acted!'*

~ Psalm 22:30–1 ~

### Prayer for Reflection

Thanks be to you, O God,
for Ninian and Columba
through whom these shores were first won for Christ.

Thanks be to you for their successors,
those named and unknown in history,
whose passion for the Gospel
    and love of the Lord
kept the flame of faith burning
even through dark and doubting years.

Thanks be to you for those in my lifetime
whose words and witness
have helped to win me for Christ.

May I honour their memory and serve my Lord
by helping others as others have helped me
to see, love, and come to Jesus.

## Prayer on Today's Theme

As once, Lord Jesus, you identified unlikely folk,
    Peter and Andrew, Martha and Mary,
    to be your ambassadors in plain clothes
    and in the common tongue,
do the same today.

Inspire not just the gifted orator to preach convincingly,
    not just the famous evangelist to win souls;
inspire the unlikely folk to lead attractive lives
    and share deep convictions
    which find their root in you.

Give us a revival not on our terms,
but in perfect keeping
with the purposes of your kingdom.

# *Evangelising*

*Go therefore to all nations ... teach them ... and make them my disciples.*

~ Matthew 28:19 ~

### Prayer for Reflection

You spoke this word to your church; you speak it now to
    me.
Am I then your evangelist, Lord?
From my reading of the Bible I am aware of the need
     to share the good news of Jesus
      and the promise of eternal life.
That *makes* me your evangelist.

### Prayer on Today's Theme

Lord God, we pray that,
as we speak to you, you will speak to us,
as we come to know you, you will speak through us to
    others,
and something of you will shine out from us
bringing others to know you as Lord and Saviour.

As Ninian, Columba, and the early saints
brought your good news to distant shores,

to a people who did not know you,
show us how to bring that same good news to our nation
    again,
for there are still many who know nothing of the love of
    Jesus Christ.

May our lives as well as our lips
say a word for Jesus,
and may something of your light
shine out from us
and bring others to know you as Lord and Saviour.

# Ecumenism

*How good and how pleasant it is to live together in unity.*

~ Psalm 133:1 ~

## Prayer for Reflection

Lord Jesus Christ,
you were neither protestant nor catholic,
neither episcopalian nor baptist,
neither conservative nor charismatic.

Labels did not hang easily on you
and you quickly removed the labels
your friends and adversaries hung on others.

Before my loyalty to my denomination,
let me always set my love for you.
Lord, I want to be a Christian in my heart.

## Prayer on Today's Theme

God of the Church
and Lord of History,
thank you for the rich traditions and proud heritage
which are the legacy of Christians who lived before us.

Now, in an era when the walls of suspicion
which divided Christian from Christian
are being broken down,
may we never be found
trying to re-erect the barriers.
Rather let all your folk be keen to discover
the lights by which others came to and keep faith.
And if anything is found which might help us
walk more closely to you
in the community of your Church,
let us receive such things gladly
as gifts of grace meant for this time in our journey.

# *Hospitality*

Lord, you only ask
that I welcome the stranger
as you have welcomed me.

For in Christ
you have brought *me*, the wanderer,
the exile, back home from the far country
into the warmth of your house,
and into the household of your people.
You have welcomed me to your table
and spread bread and wine before me.

Such welcoming grace
is the very essence of all that you are
and of all that I am called to become.

Lord, I pray for my church,
and for my part in its life.
May we be a people of warmth,

of gracious welcome,
a homely house for the exile,
a table spread in the wilderness
for the stranger and the wanderer.

## Prayer Activity

Construct a prayer place for yourself. This might be a corner in a room, an attic, or wherever. In this special corner put photographs or other reminders of people for whom you pray. When you go there, imagine that you are welcoming them into the circle of your prayer.

# Communion (1)

*At daybreak he departed and went into a deserted place.*

~ Luke 4:42 ~

### Prayer for Ourselves

Jesus found the need to withdraw,
to a quiet place, to be alone, to commune with God.
He would return with a clearer vision of the tasks that
    awaited him,
and a renewed strength
to carry them out.

How much more do I need these times, Lord, to glimpse
    your vision,
to be equipped for your service.
Forgive me when I become so busy
that I hardly give you the time of day.

### Prayer for Others

We pray for those who are always rushing about,
anxious if they have nothing to do,
well-meaning but sometimes misguided.

We pray for those whose duties are so taxing
that they cannot stop and think.
We pray for those at the beck and call of others,
who have no time to themselves.
Stop them all in their tracks before it is too late
and they lose touch with themselves and, Lord, with you
   also.

Give to us, O Lord, a quiet mind,
furnished with peaceful thoughts,
patient words and gentle deeds.
May we have a lively faith,
   a firm hope and fervent love.
Take from us all lukewarmness of spirit
   and all dullness in prayer,
and grant that we may labour
   for that which we ask of you;
through Jesus Christ our Lord.   AMEN.

~ *Thomas More (1478–1535)* ~

# Communion (2)

I give thanks for the beauty of the trees around me.
As I listen to the feelings evoked in me by trees I feel joy,
    exuberance and delight
And feel connected with trees clapping their hands,
All creation praising you and uplifting me
When I listen.

When I brush under natural arches I feel welcomed,
    affirmed and special.
When I walk in a cathedral of trees I rejoice.
Feeling deep connection with these trees that have been
    here for several generations,
Spanning time and still living,
Speaking to me of beauty, life and growth even across
    centuries,
And of your faithfulness to us in a cycle of nature that
    continues
Year after year
Nourishment and beauty intermingled.

And connection with people from Biblical times who like
   me rejoiced with trees
And connection with people who built cathedrals
Embodying, reflecting trees.

Keep us vigilant, Lord, to listen to nature around us
Keep us aware of the delicate balance now imperilled
Keep us from further abuse of the interconnectedness that
   gives us life.   AMEN.

### Readings

| | |
|---|---|
| Judges 9:6–15 | *A wisdom story about trees* |
| 1 Kings 6:29–36 | *Trees in the fabric and design of the Temple* |
| Isaiah 55:9–13 | *Joy, peace and praise in all creation* |
| Luke 21:29–38 | *Jesus invites us to listen and learn from trees* |

### Prayer Activity

Look at a tree. Notice qualities which it embodies: strength, flexibility, colour, shape. Allow these qualities to be present within you, flowing between you and the tree; rejoice in this communion with God's creation and let words of prayer flow.

# The Sacraments

*... and when he had given thanks, he broke it and said, 'This is my body ...'*

~ 1 Corinthians 11:24 ~

God who reaches out for us, how can we know you better?
There are the Scripture stories, a great read, convincing,
  often moving,
making us want to believe and to follow.
There are the doctrines, often, it's true, read from between
  the lines,
developed in dialogue and in prayer over centuries, making
  sense of life in God,
giving us a faith we can discuss and share.

Yet, Lord, you give us more to go on.
For at times in your earthly life you reached out and
  embraced us within your own life, giving us a direct line
  that remains open even now.
Your very own waters of baptism drench us;
in cup and bread you put the taste of servanthood in our
  mouths.
You invite us, Take and eat; you command us, Go and
  baptise.

Taking the ordinary things that sustain our lives
– word, water, wine and bread –
you renew us in mind, in body and in spirit,
and show in us before the whole world what true
    community can mean.
We pray for our broken communities, where sharing is
    fraught with danger;
for places of religious or ethnic conflict,
where the holy things only help determine who is the
    enemy;
when the ordinary things of life are squandered, so that
    there is no water to bless,
no bread to pass, and the cup is empty.
Help us all to see the things and people around us not as
    there for our disposal
but as bearers of messages from you, sacraments to call us
    to abundant life.

### Readings

Isaiah 25:6–10  *The feast for all peoples*
Mark 1:4–11  *The baptism by John*
John 21:9–14  *A meal with the Risen Christ*

### Prayer Activity

Take two ordinary objects, one a piece of bread or a container
of water, the other quite different – a pebble, a carving, a
picture, a household object. Reflect on how the bread or
the water becomes sacramental, a sign taking us directly to
the side of Christ. Then reflect on the other object, and ask
yourself in what way it also speaks of God and conveys God's
life to you.

# The Scriptures

*Thy word is a lamp to my feet and a light to my path.*
~ Psalm 119:105 ~

O Lord God we thank you for the Scriptures –
    its thrilling stories of high adventure,
    its poetry that touches and lifts the heart,
    its disturbing and challenging prophecy,
    its letters of encouragement and exhortation,
    its strange and wonderful visions,
and above all its telling of Jesus: the Word made flesh.
We bless you that in the Scriptures
all human life is there, and your life is there for us
    to comfort and chastise and console us,
    to direct us to Christ and the everlasting way.

O God, who inspired people to record
your royal law, your lively oracles,
help us not only to read our Bible
but to discern its imperishable truth,
to hear your word in its words and to be enriched in every
    way.

O God, we remember
all who translate the Good Book,
all who publish the Scriptures,
all who disseminate the Bible,
all who study and interpret it,
all who proclaim your Word in it.
We pray for ourselves
as we try to live by its precepts
and trust and follow the Word that is Christ.    AMEN.

# Jonah

*But Jonah set out to flee to Tarshish from the presence of the Lord.*

~ Jonah 1:3 ~

Lord, is this not a picture of ourselves,
a picture of your church?
Are we not Jonah?
Called, commissioned, appointed
to be your instruments, your channels in the world?

So often we deny the calling;
we flee from our appointing;
we turn from the task in fear,
rushing off in our own chosen direction,
and finding ourselves in the cavernous dark place of our
    own failure.

But even there –
perhaps especially there –
you enable us to hear the Word
that is our release from captivity:
'come, follow me'.
Help us to do so today.

## Prayer Activity

Begin making a time-line, a map of your own life's journey, marking key events and experiences. Focus on one place where God has met with you and perhaps changed the course of your journey. Allow this reflection to become a prayer of thanksgiving.

# *Drowning*

*Then the Lord spoke to the fish, and it spewed Jonah out upon the dry land.*

~ Jonah 2:10 ~

Lord,
Out of the dark place,
Out of the constricting place,
Out of the disturbing place,

Jonah was re-born,
Given back life,
Given back hope,
Given back purpose.

From the depths,
He returned to the surface.
From his fear
He was released for faith.

In Jonah, you show me

That

Even in my rebellion –
Even in my disobedience
Even in my fear

I can be re-born into life and hope.

Today I pray for the Church:
So often imprisoned in fear
And held fast in the grip
Of remembered failure ...

Show us, Lord,
That even our fear and failure
Can become the womb
From which a new day is born.

### Prayer Activity

Jonah was 'imprisoned' in the belly of the great fish. (Some biblical scholars have taken this to be a symbol of the deportation to Babylon which 'swallowed up' the Jews when Jerusalem was destroyed in 587 BC.) Make a collection of cuttings of prisoners of conscience. Place these in your prayer corner and use them as a focus for prayer.

# The People of Babel

One language, yet we cannot understand each other;
one God, yet we cannot worship as one;
one world, yet we cannot live together.

Holy God, with truth,
bring a little confusion to our well-ordered theology that
    has us at each other's throats;
with grace,
bring a little chaos to the exclusive orthodoxy that divides
    us;
with love,
bring a little disorder to the ingrained traditions that
    prevent us from meeting each other.

And may we find the space to pray:
for those who live with division,
for those who cannot get along,
for those who arrive at conflict too easily,
and for those who do not understand.

One language,
and may we praise you with it; one God,
and may we adventure together; one world,
and may we share it lovingly.

## Prayer Activity

Reflect on an image of a tree and all its branches tangled
together. Yet in this entanglement lies its beauty. Or consider
a photograph of a range of mountains and its cragginess. In
your mind, draw out its beauty from the roughness. Reflect
finally on the confusions that may lie within your own life,
and offer yourself space to look more from the eyes of God
and imagine the deep-down beauty that God sees. Share in
that encouragement.

# The Levites

*At that time the Lord set apart the tribe of Levi to carry the ark of the covenant of the Lord, to stand before the Lord to minister to him, and to bless in his name, to this day.*

~ Deuteronomy 10:8 ~

Lord, they were the professionals,
the temple administrators, the religious establishment.

Descended from Aaron, they had a lofty pedigree
as those charged with guarding the Law and
communicating the Faith to the people.

Yet how easily the system took over.
That which should have liberated people for living became
a constricting cage of conformity.
That which should have eased the burden added ever
greater loads to weary shoulders.
In its rigidity and its fear-driven defensiveness,
the establishment became a bulwark against the Kingdom,
a solid wall against change and newness.
It became an attempt to pin down the God who is very
Spirit and Life.

Lord, I pray for your Church
that has so often gone the same way as the Temple and its
   officials.
I pray for those who are called to proclaim the Word and to
   break the bread and pour the wine.
I pray for all who are charged with caring for the Church
   and maintaining its life and witness in the community.
I pray for my own congregation and my part in it.

### Prayer Activity

In your prayer corner set two things: a dead twig and a
flowering plant. Sit in silence, looking at these objects. Ask
yourself: what is the 'dead wood' in my life that needs to be
discarded? Old resentments? Guilt? Prejudices? Offer these
to God. What are the signs of newness and fruitfulness in
my life? Where is my life 'blossoming'? Give thanks to God
for these signs of life.

# Philistines

*'Do not cease to cry out to the Lord our God for us, and pray that he may save us from the hand of the Philistines.'*

~ 1 Samuel 7:8 ~

Lord, how do we know who your enemies are?
Were the Philistines really beyond the pale?
Were they not defending their land and livelihood? Are
  they not more like us than we allow?
No-one likes Philistines.
For us they have become a byword;
they cause opera houses to close,
believe function comes before beauty;
anyway, that's the way we see them.
But might we be seeing an expression of a different culture,
  rather than no culture at all?

Lord, we are not only content to be right;
the other person has to be wrong.
As nations, we need others who are not us so that we have
  an identity to cling to.
Save us from demonising whole peoples just because we
  need there to be a difference between them and us,

so that when we consume, when we hoard, we can say:
   'Because we're worth it!
We need have no conscience about these others!'

Help us, Lord, not to use culture or custom
as a means of identity, defining who we are,
but to slip as effortlessly as Christ
into the lives and lifestyles of others,
at home with them, one family.
Give us the generosity that offers all we have,
as Christ gave all for us.

## Prayer Activity

Do you know people from another country or culture? Or
from another part of the country now in your community or
church? Think of one of them. Ask what makes him or her
different from you. Then ask if there is anything you have
in common.

# Crowds around Jesus

*When he saw the crowds, he had compassion for them, because they were harassed and helpless, like sheep without a shepherd.*

~ Matthew 9:36 ~

Lord Jesus, you knew all about crowds:
    you moved among them, you taught and healed them,
      you fed them even;
    they were often captivated by you:
    amazed at what you did, in awe of your authority,
      impressed by your words.
As we in our day sense you,
    may any fascination turn into faith, any wonder turn
      into worship.
As we hear you speak may we, like many long ago, hear
  you gladly,
    and may we acclaim you as the Palm Sunday crowd
      acclaimed you.
    Son of David, help us to go with the crowd, such a
      crowd as shouted 'Hosanna!'
Lord Jesus, you knew all about crowds:
    that other crowd who came with swords and clubs to
      arrest you,

that other crowd who replied to Pilate's question as to
what he might do,
that crowd which shrieked 'Crucify! ... His blood be
on us!'
Save us from going with such crowds:
those who in blood-lust seek supposed retribution,
those who shout in nationalistic malice or sing some
chauvinistic sinister song,
those who watching some exciting game express bitter
bigotry in chant or chorus.
We pray for situations where men and women meet in
large numbers:
political demonstrations ... football matches ... pop
festivals ... evangelistic meetings ...
may there be enthusiasm with sense, excitement without
danger, enjoyment unalloyed.
Lord Jesus, we pray for crowds and for ourselves when we
might be in them.
Let not panic take a grip, with folk creating their own
disaster.
So may they and we come to that crowd that no one can
number
who see you face to face in the Father's House.   AMEN.

# *Disciples*

*And Jesus said to them, 'Follow me and I will make you fish for people.'*
*And immediately they left their nets and followed him.*

~ Mark 1:17–18 ~

Lord Jesus, you said 'Follow me' and they did;
the twelve chosen to be your closest disciples, and others,
    adding their experience to the group.

Today we reflect on this assortment of people from
    everyday walks of life,
none of them highly educated or religious, nothing
    particularly special about them.

Yet, Lord, you saw their potential;
you saw past the labels of tax-collector and fisherman,
you saw in them what they could and would be.

It would have been wonderful to be a fly on the wall
listening to all their conversations and discussions:
what did they speak about in private?
were they always serious?
did they have a laugh every now and then?
what were their private thoughts about you, Jesus, whom
    they followed?

You see the potential in each of us and call us to 'come and follow'.

Help us to leave everything behind and immediately follow you, today and every day.

### Readings

| | |
|---:|:---|
| Mark 1:16–20 | *Calling of the first disciples* |
| Matthew 10:1–15 | *The twelve disciples' mission* |
| John 8:31–59 | *True disciples* |

### Prayer Activity

The disciples were fortunate in that they could speak to Jesus in person, face to face. Close your eyes and imagine that you are sitting with Jesus. Is there something you would like to talk to him about? Tell him now and sit quietly, enjoying being in his presence.

# *Calling*

*And Jesus said to them, 'Follow me and I will make you fish for
people.'*

~ Mark 1:17 ~

Where the waves lapped against the shore,
as salty, sandy hands tugged at nets and slippery fish,
when the working day was in full swing,
Jesus came, and the familiar was soon cast aside.

And yet, God, it seems so absurd that those men downed
  tools and followed your son.

What convinced them?
What made them leave so much and take up so much?
Today we, too, grapple with that challenge.

So help us recognise that compelling communication you
  had and have with your people,
for in Jesus you spoke to the heart of working
  communities;
farmers and fishers, those who worked with their hands;
you spoke and they understood beyond words,
hearing you the maker and the worker of wonders.

So that's the call to us today too, typists and teachers,
scientists and social workers ...

Maybe not to down tools ...
but to bring your transforming presence into what we are
already doing.

To notice that, as we teach – we hear the patience of Jesus,
As we write – we know the creativity of Spirit,
As we care – we nurture your compassion,
As we make and communicate and order – we begin
again our journey where something in you overwhelms
something in us,
making us follow no matter what or where.

### Prayer Activity

Reflect on three very different ways people earn a living, for
example, by working with their hands as a joiner or builder,
using their minds as researcher or technician or by expressing
creativity as designer or artist. How might God speak to them
in these tasks? What do you do that links you to the nature
of God without words and what qualities from God do you
need to work today?

# Discipleship

*My Father is glorified by this, that you bear much fruit and become my disciples.*

~ John 15:8 ~

## Prayer for Ourselves

I know the warmth of your love in my life, Lord,
and want to bear fruit that will bring you glory,
but I know there may need to be painful pruning
if the fruit I bear is to be good fruit.
I lay my life before you, the Gardener.
Help me not to regret what you cut away
or resent what you rearrange
but to welcome your tending of me
that I may grace your garden
and be a refreshment for others.

## Prayer for Others

We pray for those who have been hurt and bruised,
those who have not been able
to grow to their full potential,
those who have yet to mature,
to blossom and bear fruit,

those in younger years
that all their vitality and energy
may not go unharvested,
those who are weary in well doing
who feel their efforts come to nothing,
those who work hard
but do not see the fruits of their labours,
those who labour but to little purpose,
those who claim too much
for what they are able to produce.

# Fellowship

*God is faithful; by him you were called into the fellowship of his Son, Jesus Christ our Lord.*

~ 1 Corinthians 1:9 ~

## Prayer for Ourselves

When you created us, God,
you created us for fellowship with you.
Even when I want to hide from you,
    you come looking for me;
in Christ you brought me back
    into your company.

But I am not your only child, Lord.
For in Jesus also you reconciled
all people to yourself
and made us for each other,
living in a community of love.

When I try to live as if you don't matter,
or as if I am the only person in the world,
call me back to you
and bring me face to face with my neighbour.

## Prayer for Others

Hear our prayers, Lord,
for those who have wandered from you,
for those who are searching for you,
for those who have a restlessness,
  that they may find rest and peace in you.
Hear our prayers, Lord,
for those who have broken fellowship with others,
those who try to go it alone,
that they might realise how much they need you, and need
 others too.

He bids us build each other up;
and gathered into one,
to our high calling's glorious hope
we hand in hand go on.

 ~ *Charles Wesley (1707–88)* ~

# Defending the Faith

*Always be ready to make your defence when anyone challenges you to justify the hope that is in you.*

~ 1 Peter 3:15 ~

## Prayer for Reflection

Thank you, Lord,
for this clear mandate to witness to you,
    wherever I am,
    whoever I'm with,
    at all times, to all people.

But this is not a licence to browbeat,
to bludgeon people into believing
    with loquacious monologues
    and an insufferable goodness.

Help me rather to treasure the Good News in my heart,
    my life, and my conversation,
that others may recognise what their hearts yearn for
    and what their lives desperately seek.

### Prayer on Today's Theme

Remember, Lord,
those whose responsibility is to defend the faith,
scholars, monarchs, preachers, religious broadcasters,
who must ever find new words to touch the heart,
new styles of presentation to arrest the attention,
ever-renewed conviction to persevere in their task.

I pray for those lost for lack of a faith,
those who cling to an immature faith
    which one day will not stand the test,
those who feel on the fringes of faith
      but put off finding out more
      or who are put off by the Christians they know.

Renew your Church, Lord,
      until it unmistakably can declare
      in whom it lives and moves.

# Martyrs

When they heard these things, they became enraged and ground their
teeth at Stephen. But filled with the Holy Spirit, he gazed into heaven
and saw the glory of God.

~ Acts 7:54–5 ~

'Glorious things of thee are spoken', the ancient hymn
    declares,
and yet, God, terrible things have been done to those who
    declared your name.

We wrestle today with the thought of dying for our beliefs,
    with the idea of suffering for our faith, being persecuted
    to death.
For we are of a world that often believes nothing and that
    at best mocks
or has pity on those with passion and the courage of
    conviction.

So may we reflect now on those from the Bible who faced
    rage head on,
who did not back down but kept on proclaiming and who
    in pain, with death approaching,
remembered Christ, and with faith, in reverence and
    complete surrender to your cause of love, cried: 'Lord,
    receive my spirit, do not hold this sin against them.'

As we recall that group of biblical martyrs
who let their lives end for your glory to shine through,
let us learn how to stand strong and make our lives count
   for Christ in this day.
Let us pray for those who boldly go and suffer the
   consequences
– who do things we would never do for the gospel.
But above all, let us regain and relive the passion of Christ,
   love that is the be-all and end-all,
and glimpses of resurrection that bring life to our dead
   places,
colour and experience and courage behind our locked
   doors.

### Prayer Activity

Scared? What of? Of whom? Let Jesus receive these fears and
anxieties from you, and ask him what he would do.

# Faith – a Man Struggles with Belief

*'I believe; help my unbelief!'*
~ Mark 9:24 ~

Lord of faith, so often I struggle with what to believe:
the loose ends,
the unanswered questions,
the eternal 'Why?'
Too often I have little to say to those who ask
and find myself with the same doubts.
Why this tragedy?
Why that death?
Why the unfairness?
Why the disappointment?

I believe, but help my unbelief!

When I struggle with things too great,
when I feel unequal to the task,
when I reel from blows,
when the world goes dark,
take me by the hand, lift me up, that I may arise
and see the brightness of a new day, the colours of creation,
the power of faith at work.

For me, and for all who struggle with their faith,
bring that touch of belief which banishes the shadow of
   doubt,
that I may see, that I may believe.   AMEN.

## Readings

Psalm 22
Psalm 27
Psalm 42
Mark 9:14–29
2 Corinthians 4:6–18
2 Corinthians 12:7–10

## Prayer Activity

Let all the waves of your emotions have their full effect. Notice
the most dominant emotion within you at this moment.
Whether you are joyful or very sad, let the emotions flow over
you like a waterfall. Value your emotions, experience them
as fluid and flowing – bring life, energy and sparkle – like a
waterfall. Let go and let God show you what to do next, how
to allow the emotions to flow.

# Commitment

*Commit your ways to the Lord; trust in him and he will act.*

~ Psalm 37:5 ~

## Prayer for Reflection

In imitation of my Saviour,
this day I commit into your hands, O God,
     my deepest hope, my greatest fear,
     my fondest friend, my farthest adversary,
     my health, my conversation,
     my wealth, my imagination,
     my life, my love,
     my spirit.

Do not cradle me gently as if I were not meant for this
    world;
rather hold me firmly
that I may be faithful in my commitment to you
and to all your people.

## Prayer on Today's Theme

Today I remember, Lord,
those who have yet to throw in their lot with you.

Some enjoy talking about you,
but would not risk talking to you.
Some should be close by your side,
but the wrong word at the right time
 from one of your followers
 has kept them at arm's length.
Some are aflame with great ideas,
but have yet to find the bridge
 from conviction to commitment.

For them I pray,
and for all who dither on the doorstep of discipleship,
that they may not fear to turn and face you
 or take your hand
 which is calloused with care.

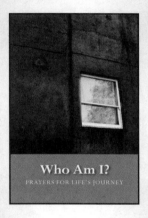